What Every Teacher Should Know About
Student Motivation

What Every Teacher Should Know About...

What Every Teacher Should Know About
Diverse Learners

What Every Teacher Should Know About
Student Motivation

What Every Teacher Should Know About
Learning, Memory, and the Brain

What Every Teacher Should Know About
Instructional Planning

What Every Teacher Should Know About
Effective Teaching Strategies

What Every Teacher Should Know About
Classroom Management and Discipline

What Every Teacher Should Know About
Student Assessment

What Every Teacher Should Know About
Special Learners

What Every Teacher Should Know About
Media and Technology

What Every Teacher Should Know About
The Profession and Politics of Teaching

DONNA WALKER TILESTON

What Every Teacher Should Know About
Student Motivation

CORWIN PRESS
A Sage Publications Company
Thousand Oaks, California

For information:

Corwin Press
A Sage Publications Company
2455 Teller Road
Thousand Oaks, California 91320
www.corwinpress.com

Sage Publications Ltd.
6 Bonhill Street
London EC2A 4PU
United Kingdom

Sage Publications India Pvt. Ltd.
B-42, Panchsheel Enclave
Post Box 4109
New Delhi 110 017 India

Printed in the United States of America

Library of Congress Cataloging-in-Publication Data

Tileston, Donna Walker.
What every teacher should know about student motivation / Donna Walker Tileston.
    p. cm. — (What every teacher should know about— ; 2)
Includes bibliographical references and index.
    ISBN 0-7619-3118-X (pbk.)
1. Motivation in education. 2. Teacher-student relationships.
I. Title II. Series: Tileston, Donna Walker. What every teacher should know about—2.
LB1065.T56 2004
370.15′4—dc21   2003010238

This book is printed on acid-free paper.

04   05   06   10   9   8   7   6   5   4   3

Acquisitions Editor:	Faye Zucker
Editorial Assistant:	Stacy Wagner
Production Editor:	Diane S. Foster
Copy Editor:	Stacey Shimizu
Typesetter:	C&M Digitals (P) Ltd.
Proofreader:	Mary Meagher
Indexer:	Molly Hall
Cover Designer:	Tracy E. Miller
Production Artist:	Lisa Miller

Contents

About the Author

Donna Walker Tileston, Ed.D., is a veteran teacher of 27 years and the president of Strategic Teaching and Learning, a consulting firm that provides services to schools throughout the United States and Canada. Also an author, Donna's publications include *Strategies for Teaching Differently: On the Block or Not* (Corwin Press, 1998), *Innovative Strategies of the Block Schedule* (Bureau of Education and Research [BER], 1999), and *Ten Best Teaching Practices: How Brain Research, Learning Styles, and Standards Define Teaching Competencies* (Corwin Press, 2000), which has been on Corwin's best-seller list since its first year in print.

Donna received her B.A. from the University of North Texas, her M.A. from East Texas State University, and her Ed.D. from Texas A & M University-Commerce. She may be reached at www.strategicteachinglearning.com or by e-mail at dwtileston@yahoo.com.

Acknowledgments

My sincere thanks go to my Acquisitions Editor, Faye Zucker, for her faith in education and what this information can do to help all children be successful. Without Faye, these books would not have been possible.

I had the best team of editors around: Diane Foster, Stacy Wagner, and Stacey Shimizu. You took my words and you gave them power. Thank you.

Thanks to my wonderful Board Chairman at Strategic Teaching and Learning, Dulany Howland: Thank you for sticking with me in the good times and the tough spots. Your expertise and friendship have been invaluable.

*To my friends and board members, Vicki and Dulany Howland,
who have encouraged me throughout this project.*

Introduction

What a wonderful time to be a teacher! Never before have we had available to us the answers to unlock the mysteries of the mind or to change the world in the way that we have at this time. Through brain research and its implications for learning and remembering, we truly have the tools to work smarter. Never before have we had the opportunity to make positive change in today's troubled classrooms that we have today.

You have chosen one of the most awesome professions on earth; you have chosen to be a teacher. John Steinbeck wrote a wonderful poem, "Like Captured Butterflies," about a teacher who touched his soul. She was the kind of teacher who created a love of learning within her students. As teachers, we can choose to join those who punch in and out each day to receive a paycheck and who teach what Steinbeck called "soon forgotten things," or we can choose to be the kind of teacher who "creates a new hunger" for learning in students' minds. I have written this program for those of us who have chosen the latter path.

For so long we have been told to emphasize the cognitive system of the brain. As teachers, we often begin our lessons by teaching for cognitive knowledge and then for processes. No wonder our students are sleeping in class! They come from a multimedia world, a world in which they receive instant feedback and gratification through games, through the Internet, and through sports. They come to our classrooms to sit and listen passively without giving any forethought to why they are learning information of civilizations long ago or math equations or grammar. We now know, thanks to the work of people like Marzano (1992, 1998, 2001), Jensen (1997, 1998), Sylwester (1995), and others that learning does not begin with the cognitive system of the brain. Rather, learning begins in the self-system of the brain, and it is this system that decides whether the learning is worthy of our attention.

In this book, you will find a map to guide you to activating motivation in your students.

Since one of the most effective ways that we can teach vocabulary to our students is to introduce the vocabulary, have our students provide their own ideas about what the words mean, and then guide them to examine the meanings in context, the following exercise is offered. Form 0.1 provides the vocabulary that will be examined throughout this book. Look at the words to see which ones are familiar and which are not. Write your own definitions in the middle column, and adjust your thinking as you read through this book.

In addition, I am providing a vocabulary pre-test for you. After you have read the book, you will be given a post-test and the solutions to the tests. The Vocabulary Summary offers additional information about these words and other terms associated with motivation.

Form 0.1   Vocabulary List for Student Motivation

Vocabulary Word	Your Definition	Your Revised Definition
At-risk students		
Celebrations		
Climate		
Contextualization		
Extrinsic motivation		
Feedback		
Generational poverty		
Intrinsic motivation		
Learned helplessness		
Learning state		
Locus of control		
Metacognitive system		
Off-task behavior		
Rewards		
Self-efficacy		
Self-esteem		
Self-system		
Self-talk		
Teacher expectations		
Threat		
Wait time		

Vocabulary Pre-Test

I nstructions: Choose the one best answer for each of the questions provided.

1. Students who come to the classroom believing that nothing they do will be successful have most likely acquired . . .
   A. Locus of control
   B. Learned helplessness
   C. Meaning making
   D. Affective domain

2. Which of the following control initial motivation to listen to the teacher?
   A. Locus of control
   B. Metacognitive system
   C. Potential embarrassment
   D. Self-system

3. When a student perceives that he or she can be successful based on past success, this is an example of . . .
   A. Extrinsic motivation
   B. Positive reinforcement
   C. Self-efficacy
   D. Meaning making

4. Which of the following learning states are *not* desirable?
   A. Suspense
   B. High anxiety

C. High challenge

D. Temporary confusion

5. Which of the choices below is an example of cultural/social threat?

   A. Physical harm

   B. Potential embarrassment

   C. Disrespect

   D. Unreasonable deadlines

6. Which of the choices below is an example of intellectual threat?

   A. Disrespect

   B. Unreasonable deadlines

   C. Incomplete directions given for a task

   D. Working by oneself

7. Self-efficacy is an important part of . . .

   A. Metacognition

   B. The self-system

   C. Physical needs

   D. Safety needs

8. Feedback . . .

   A. Should be positive only.

   B. Should be constructive only.

   C. Should be given in general terms such as "good job."

   D. Should be specific, positive, and constructive.

9. Which of the following is not a condition for being at risk?

   A. Previous failure

   B. Low socioeconomic status

   C. Previous discipline problems

   D. Single parent home

10. Which of the following is not true of self-talk?

    A. It is usually done aloud.

    B. It can be negative.

C. It can be positive.

D. It is linked to student success.

11. Which of the following is an example of a reward?
    A. Students are told that they will be given stickers for good work.
    B. Students are provided with stickers after they do surprisingly well on a test.
    C. Students in groups give each other high-fives for completing their work.
    D. Students are praised by the teacher for their good behavior.

12. Most off-task behavior is the result of . . .
    A. Teacher behavior
    B. Difficult tasks
    C. A poor learning state
    D. The desire for attention

13. Which of the following is an example of a celebration?
    A. Students are praised by the teacher for their good behavior.
    B. Students are promised a pizza party for good behavior.
    C. Students are given the opportunity to win a bicycle for perfect attendance.
    D. Students are promised and then given free time for good grades on the Friday test.

14. Which of the following is an example of resource restriction?
    A. An essay returned with derisive comments
    B. Isolation from peers during class
    C. An English language learner taught verbally
    D. A negative reward system

15. There are two kinds of climate in the classroom: They are . . .
    A. Isolational and inclusive
    B. Emotional and physical

C. Cultural and social

D. Physical and mental

16. Which of the following is *not* an aspect of positive feedback?
    A. It is provided at least every 30 minutes.
    B. It is sincere.
    C. It is provided frequently.
    D. It is given whether earned or not.

17. Schools which use contextualization are . . .
    A. Usually working with special needs students.
    B. Teaching students from urban poverty.
    C. Teaching to the text.
    D. Teaching gifted students.

18. Which of the following statements is true of wait time?
    A. The amount of time varies with the learners.
    B. Clues should be given to help the learner remember.
    C. Brighter students should not be given as much time as slower students.
    D. Wait time should be the same for all learners.

19. *Locus of control* refers to . . .
    A. The extent that learners can control others.
    B. The extent that others can control the learner.
    C. How much control the learner perceives that he has.
    D. The teacher's ability to maintain order.

20. *Generational poverty* refers to . . .
    A. The loss of a job by the major breadwinner of the family.
    B. The loss of jobs by several generations of members of the family.
    C. An economic status caused by homelessness.
    D. An economic status over time.

1

What Is Motivation and Why Does It Matter So Much?

Instead of asking "How can I motivate students?" a better question would be, "In what ways is the brain naturally motivated from within?"

—Eric Jensen, *Completing the Puzzle*

Most of us were trained to teach to the cognitive system of the brain. We stand before our classes to provide access to this world of knowledge for our students. Why, then, aren't they motivated to learn? After all, isn't cognitive knowledge what students must acquire to master standards, to pass state and national exams, and to be successful in school? All learning begins not in the cognitive system, but in the self-system. It happens with or without our input, but we are more likely that our students will be motivated to learn and to complete tasks when we are directly involved in the learning process from the beginning. Marzano (2001) says, "Once the self-system has determined what will be attended to, the functioning of all other elements of thought (i.e., the metacognitive system, the cognitive system, and the knowledge domains) are, to a certain extent, dedicated or determined." In this chapter, we will examine motivation and why it is crucial to learning and remembering.

Motivation relates to the drive to do something. Motivation causes us to get up in the morning and go to work. Motivation drives us to study new things, and motivation encourages us to try again when we fail. Just as there are times when you or I feel more or less motivated to do something, the same is true for our students. Think about the last time that you had to learn something that was either difficult or for which you had little personal interest. What motivated you to complete the task? When the task became difficult or when you experienced a roadblock, what caused you to complete the task?

We cannot be motivated for our students; that is something they must find for themselves. What we can do is directly teach them skills that will help them to begin a task with energy and to complete it even when it becomes difficult. Many students today have not been taught those skills. If you teach inner-city students and students from poverty, then you may teach students who have acquired responses to learning that work against the self-system of the brain. Motivation to pay attention to the learning, to begin a task, and to complete it are an innate part of the self-system and metacognitive system of the brain, and they can be activated through tactics used by the classroom teacher.

WHAT IS THE BIG DEAL
ABOUT INTRINSIC MOTIVATION?

As teachers, our goal is to guide students to use the innate drive that we all have for intrinsic motivation. Often, students who have been given external rewards—such as money, food, or stickers—for desired behavior will have less drive to do something just for the joy of doing it. Teachers can change that behavior by changing teaching tactics and by gradually weaning students from external rewards to celebrations of the learning.

As teachers, there are a variety of approaches that we can take to enhance motivation on the days that our students are feeling less motivated. Before we can create a viable plan for activating the systems of thinking in our students, it is important to understand the differences between intrinsic and extrinsic motivation.

Intrinsic motivation is the drive that comes from within; students do something for the sheer joy of doing it or because they want to discover something, answer a question, or experience the feeling of self-accomplishment.

Based on the experiences that our students bring with them to the classroom, they may or may not be intrinsically motivated. Students who grow up in an environment in which they do only those things for which they receive a tangible reward will be less intrinsically motivated. For those students, it will be more difficult to break the pattern of rewards for work—but this break *can* be accomplished with the patience and consistency of the classroom teachers involved. Brain researchers say that we are born with the tendency toward intrinsic motivation—watch a two-year-old explore the world and you will see what I mean. However, over time, if students are constantly promised rewards if they will be quiet, clean their rooms, make good grades, and so forth, they may have learned to disregard that natural intrinsic motivation in favor of tangible rewards. With inner-city students or students from poverty, the natural intrinsic motivation with which they were born may have been extinguished early in life from being with caregivers who believe that they have no control over their lives. Because they believe locus of control comes from outside sources, sources beyond their control, they may have learned early on to look to outside rewards for motivation.

Intrinsic motivation comes from within—specifically from the self- and metacognitive systems. When these systems are activated positively, students work hard for their own satisfaction in learning and doing well. The perceived value of tasks is paramount to intrinsic motivation. According to Marzano (1992), "A growing body of research indicates that when students are working on goals they themselves have set, they are more motivated and efficient, and they achieve more than they do when working to meet goals set by the teacher." Both the self-system and the metacognitive systems of the brain are built around those characteristics that lend themselves to intrinsic motivation. For example, the self-system is guided by self-concept and self-efficacy and the belief that one can achieve. The metacognitive system is built around personal goal setting and follow-through, which happen without outside rewards.

What Is Extrinsic Motivation?

Extrinsic motivation is motivation that comes about because of the promise of a tangible, marketable reward. It is the desire to do something because of the promise of or hope for a tangible result. Extrinsic motivation is a product of the behaviorist point of view, which says that we can manipulate behavior by providing rewards and/or punishments. The father of this movement is generally thought to be B. F. Skinner, who conducted many experiments in which he provided rewards for desired behavior and punishments for undesired behavior (or the absence of desired behavior). Before his death, Skinner himself said that it was foolish to think that human beings would react the same as other experimental animals. Caine and Caine (1997) add,

Behaviorism, particularly as incorporated into schools, is largely based on rewards and punishment; but these are extremely complex, not simple. A smiley sticker is not just a single reward of a single act. The use of a sticker may well influence the formation of expectations, preferences, and habits having impact far beyond any single event. Thus, a single teacher behavior may have vast, but initially invisible, consequences. One of many problems with the behaviorist approach is that it does not provide for a way to acknowledge those consequences.

WHAT IS THE DIFFERENCE BETWEEN REWARDS AND CELEBRATIONS?

Extrinsic motivation is triggered by outside sources, rather than from within. These outside forces may come in the form of a reward, such as candy, money, or stickers. Extrinsic motivation may also be a hug or pat on the back. There is nothing wrong with extrinsic motivation itself: We all work for paychecks and for recognition, for example. The problem with extrinsic rewards comes when it is the only or primary factor in motivating students to learn. One of the ways that we can distinguish between positive and negative forms of extrinsic motivation is to distinguish between *rewards* and *celebrations*. Working only for rewards can be detrimental to learning, while celebrations can have a very positive effect on the learning.

In order to be classified as a reward, two characteristics will be present: It will have commercial value and will be expected. For example, a teacher who tells her students that she will give them candy if everyone finishes their work on time is offering a reward. The students know the candy is coming if they finish their work (it is expected) and candy has commercial value. If students do well on their assignment and the teacher gives them candy, this is not considered a reward but rather a celebration, because the students did not know in advance that they were going to get the candy. In other words, they did not do the work for candy; the candy was an unexpected outcome.

This is an important distinction. Alfie Kohn (1993), in his book *Punished by Rewards*, questioned the effects of rewards on motivation, saying that rewards actually help destroy intrinsic motivation. Others have said that the rewards must escalate with the child. An elementary-aged child might do the work for stickers, but by middle school she may want money or pizza. Then by high school, what do we give her—a car?

Of course, we all do some things for rewards; most of us work for a paycheck, which we know that we are getting and which has commercial value. Students work for grades as well. The point is that we want to get students to learn because learning is fun and because it helps them to achieve—not just because they will receive an external reward.

Students who have been raised on a reward system will not immediately rely on intrinsic motivation alone. Begin with extrinsic rewards, and gradually wean them off of them by skipping a reward one time, then twice, and so forth. Make the learning fun and interesting so that students want to know the information and to discover new things.

Students from poverty are often directed toward extrinsic rewards for many of the positive things that they do, so you will need patience and time to move them gradually from rewards to becoming self-motivated to learn. To move students away from expected extrinsic rewards, use extrinsic incentives, such as celebrations, in the classroom often. Celebrate the learning with high fives, cheers, and words of praise.

The use of extrinsic motivation usually begins at a young age with a system of rewards and punishments for desired behavior or completed tasks (e.g., "If you clean your room, you may watch television for an extra hour"). When the child comes to school, this learned behavior is often reinforced in the classroom. Teachers who constantly give students candy, stickers, or other prizes for good work or behavior are reinforcing the idea that we should only work for tangible rewards.

Extrinsic motivation is closely related to a reward system. For example, a teacher might tell the class that everyone who does well on the daily test will be given a prize; students may then work harder than they normally would because the promise of a reward is offered. Parents sometimes offer their students money for good grades, and teachers may offer students free time for good behavior. All of these are examples of extrinsic motivation and are at the heart of an ongoing controversy about the effects of extrinsic rewards on the brain.

Some researchers say that the constant use of extrinsic motivators actually diminishes our internal drive, our intrinsic motivation. The overuse of rewards is a form of control. Caine and Caine (1997) state,

When rewards and punishments are controlled by others, most children are influenced to look to others for direction and answers. In fact, we now seem to have an entire generation working for the grade or rewards of an immediate and tangible nature. One consequence is that they are literally demotivated in many respects. In particular, their innate search for meaning is short-circuited.

Jensen (1997) adds,

The human brain, when motivated by reward systems, operates differently than it does when motivated intrinsically. The anxiety triggered under the reward system releases neurotransmitters, which can inhibit creativity, problem solving and recall. Rewards are manipulative—part of the old school of behaviorism; and do more harm than good in the long run.

For students who are at risk or who are underachievers, the consequences of a reliance on external motivation may be lifelong, and they may not ever fully utilize the natural intrinsic motivation controlled by the self- and metacognitive systems.

While rewards have been generally rejected as a classroom tool, there is a question of what actually constitutes a reward, and what is, rather, an *incentive*. As noted above, rewards are thought of as anything that has market value and is expected. Examples of common rewards include

1. A promise of candy if students turn their work in on time.

2. The offering of an eraser if a student will behave well in class.

3. The regular gift of a sticker to students who offer correct answers on a test.

Extrinsic incentives, unlike rewards, have no material value. Examples of incentives include

1. Free time for work well done.

2. Grades for quality work.

3. Pats on the back, thumbs up, and words of praise for good work or behavior.

Look at the following scenarios and determine if the motivation is a reward or a celebration:

1. Mrs. Matthews tells her students that, if they all do well on the spelling test, they will have pizza the next day.

2. Mrs. Matthews' students all did a great job on the paper drive for the school and she surprises them with a pizza party.

In the first scenario, Mrs. Matthews has told her students in advance that she will *reward* them if they all do well: The

Form 1.1   Reward or Celebration?

Motivation Tool	Reward (Has market value and is expected)	Celebration (May have market value or be expected, but not both)
1. Promise of prizes if students do well on state test	Has market value and is expected	
2. Students given a surprise party after doing well on the state test.		Has a market value but is not expected
3. Students told that if they will behave, they will be given free time at the end of class.		Does not have market value but is expected

receipt of the pizza is predictable and the pizza itself has market value. In the second scenario, pizza has market value, but the students did not know that they would receive pizza for doing a good job—so this is an example of a celebration. Thus, in the first scenario, the teacher is using a reward for motivation, whereas in the second scenario, the students did well on their own (i.e., through intrinsic motivation) and the pizza is a celebration.

The chart in Form 1.1 may be helpful as you determine whether or not you are relying on rewards for motivation.

Remember, to be a reward, the tactic must have both market value and students must know in advance that something is being offered. To be a celebration, the tactic can have either market value or expectation, but not both. It may also have neither market value nor expectations—just be a spontaneous celebration of the learning.

2

What Are the Roots of Motivation?

I n his book *Designing a New Taxonomy of Educational Objectives* (2001), Marzano discusses motivation in terms of three systems of mental processing. In order to understand how motivation works within these systems of thinking, let's look at a seventh-grade language arts classroom as class begins.

As the language arts classroom fills with students for the beginning of the school day, the teacher, Malcolm Trevino, stands before the students to begin a new unit of study. Some students are still arranging their desks, some are looking for their books, some are staring out the window, and some are talking. Within a matter of seconds, each student's self-system will decide whether to engage in the learning—the new task— or to continue what they are doing. Here is a brief explanation of what will happen within the brains of the students.

The self-system is the prime determiner of the motivation that is brought to the new task. Marzano (2001) says,

If the task is judged important, if the probability of success is high, and a positive effect is generated or associated with the task, students will be motivated to engage in the new task. If the new task is evaluated as having low relevance and/or low probability of success and has an associated negative affect, motivation to engage in the task will be low.

This means that to be motivated, a set of beliefs must be in place. First, the students must believe that the new learning is important, and they must believe that they have the resources necessary to be successful. The students also need to have a positive feeling about the class itself. All of these things do not necessarily have equal weight, but where there is a negative belief about one of the aspects of the system, there needs to be overriding positives in the others. For example, if a student does not see the importance of learning about slope in math class, but feels comfortable and accepted in the classroom and has had positive experiences with math previously, that student is more likely to be motivated to learn slope.

There are four components of the self-system thinking that directly relate to motivation to learn; we will look at them in the next section.

How Does the Self-System Work?

While most of us use the self-system of the brain uncon-sciously, this system is at work anytime we are in a learning situation. The processes of the self-system determine whether we will engage in the learning and how much energy or enthusiasm we will bring to the event. In order to understand how this system works, let's examine the processes that are activated within the self-system as it examines the importance of an activity, our sense of efficacy, our emotional response to a task, and our overall motivation.

Examining Importance

We pay attention to those things that we consider to be important. For something to be important to us, it will usually be perceived either as instrumental in satisfying a basic need or as instrumental in the attainment of a personal goal. According to Maslow (1968),

> Human beings have evolutionarily designed needs that might even exist in somewhat of a hierarchic structure, in which needs such as physical safety, food and shelter are more basic than needs such as companionship and acceptance. If a specific knowledge component is perceived as being instrumental in meeting one or more of those needs, it will be considered important by an individual.

For example, if a student perceives that learning multiplication facts will help keep him from being cheated on the street, he may be more interested in learning multiplication facts. My favorite math teacher has a sign in her classroom that reads, "I promise that I will never teach you anything in this classroom unless I can tell you the real-world application." She teaches higher-level math, and her students do challenge her on this statement at times. She not only can tell them how it applies in the real world, she usually shows them. When students were studying slope, for example, she asked the Special Education Director to talk to her class about handicap ramps in regard to specifications and law. Then she assigned her students to measure, in small groups, the handicap ramps around the school and in the community to see if they met the specifications. (By the way, they did not all meet the specifications.) Those students who ask us, "When are we ever going to use this stuff?" are operating on a need-to-know basis: If they do not need to know it for the test on Friday or for an immediate personal goal, they may not perceive the information as relevant, and information that is not seen as relevant is discarded by the brain. Students feel overloaded by all that they must learn already, and then schools throw in mandatory testing to raise the anxiety level even more. Provide your students with the objectives for what you are studying (based on national and state standards). Put the objectives up in the room where students can see them and refer to them often throughout a unit of study so that students can see their progress. If you teach students too young to read, send a letter home telling parents what you will be doing and tie that to your state, national, and local standards. This says to students that the learning is important and that there is a plan for growth for the student.

Examining Efficacy

The extent to which individuals believe that they have the resources, ability, or power to change a situation based on past experiences is important to motivation. If a student does not believe that she has the requisite ability, resources, or power to be successful in the new task, then this will greatly lessen her motivation to try. Self-efficacy refers to the confidence a person has that he or she has the ability to be successful. The basic difference between self-efficacy and self-esteem is that, while both terms refer to students' belief that they can be successful, self-efficacy is based on past experience. A student knows he can be successful because past experience has taught him so; he knows that success is connected to effort.

The old adage "success breeds success" is absolutely true. Provide opportunities for students to experience success in incremental steps and provide specific feedback to help them improve. General statements like "good job" do not have a strong impact on learning. Students need specific feedback that is given often and consistently. They need to know what they are doing well and where they need improvement. The Mid-continent Regional Education Laboratory (McREL) conducted studies to determine which instructional practices make the most difference in student achievement. Through meta-analysis, they were able to predict how much difference in terms of percentile improvement a practice would have on an "average student" at the 50th percentile range. For example, a student working at the 50th percentile on an activity can be moved to the 77th percentile when "focused and accurate" praise was used "as the vehicle for enhancing students' beliefs about themselves relative to accomplishing specific tasks" (Marzano, 1998).

Several years ago, I was involved in a restructuring project in a high school where over 50% of the students qualified for free or reduced meals. The test scores were mediocre and the climate was negative. After a great deal of training and meetings, it was decided by the whole faculty in a vote that they would begin the new school year with a positive attitude toward students and would incorporate information on emotion and learning into the classroom. One of the tactics that the staff used was to tell students that they could be successful—even if they had not been in the past. That was reinforced daily through encouraging remarks, consistency in grading, treating students with respect, and having high expectations in every classroom. Within two months, scores were going up and parents were calling to say, "What are you doing differently? My kid loves school!" A student who had moved in from another state told me she had not done well in her former school but, she said, "You can't fail here—they just won't let you."

Examining Emotional Response

Emotion is thought to be the strongest force in the brain. Negative emotion can literally shut down thought processes, while positive emotions can help shape our motivation to learn. Don't believe me? Next time you lose your car keys, see if you can do higher-level math in your emotional state. The emotional response that a student brings to the new task will help shape the degree of motivation associated with that task. This is just one of the reasons that it is important to have a positive learning environment prior to teaching a lesson. A positive learning environment includes both the physical and emotional structures in place. A warm and caring teacher who has no consistency or planning will have difficulty in terms of student progress.

Examining Overall Motivation

According to Marzano (2001), high motivation exists when students see the information or task as personally relevant and believe that they can be successful. In contrast, a classroom where the individual does not see the purpose in the learning, does not believe he or she can be successful, and/or has a negative feeling about the teacher or class, tends to lead to demotivation.

THE METACOGNITIVE SYSTEM

Once a student decides to pay attention to the learning, the metacognitive system becomes engaged. The metacognitive system is controlled by the self-system. Once the self-system sees the learning as important, believes that the learning can be done successfully, and has a positive feeling about the learning, then the learning is passed to the metacognitive system. The metacognitive system then sets personal goals for the learning, makes decisions about what to do when problems with the task are encountered, and pushes us to complete a task with high energy.

Our sense of self and our attitudes toward the learning from the self-system affect how successful we will be as we work through the metacognitive system. For example, a student who has low self-efficacy or who has negative feelings about the learning to begin with may give up when problems are encountered. Students who have never been taught how to monitor and adjust their own learning may also exhibit impulsivity at this time. Students need to be taught specific strategies for goal setting and for how to redirect goals when problems occur. One of the ways that we do this is by teaching students positive self-talk and by demonstrating to them how we use self-talk to help us solve problems. Once the metacognitive system is engaged, it is in communication with the third system, the cognitive system.

THE COGNITIVE SYSTEM

The cognitive system is responsible for helping students process the information that they will need to complete the tasks at hand. It is responsible for such operations as making

Figure 2.1   The Three Systems of Thinking

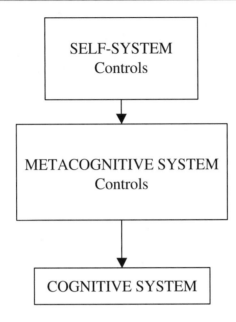

inferences, comparing, and classifying. The information that the students bring to the classroom will have an impact on their success in learning, and so we should ask, "What do my students already know and understand that will be helpful as I help them activate their innate desire to know?"

Anytime that we present students with new learning or new tasks, the brain looks for existing connections in the brain that are based on prior experiences and prior learning. If such connections are found, the new information can be connected to them. For that reason, one of the most powerful teaching strategies that we can employ in the classroom is to connect new learning to what students already know and understand. Marzano (1998) says that this is one of the most important tactics for helping students to be successful.

The model in Figure 2.1 demonstrates the relationship between the three systems discussed here and acquiring knowledge. To gain control of the cognitive system (knowledge), we must find ways to involve the metacognitive system (Marzano, 2001).

3

Motivation to Begin a Lesson or Task

C learly, we have seen that the self-system of the brain is the gatekeeper to motivation. How, then, can we gain access to this powerful system, and how can we help students to stay motivated throughout the task? Let's briefly revisit the self-system of the brain and add what is known from neuroscience in regard to paying attention and following through.

Most of what we learn comes to us through the five senses. Since the brain cannot possibly pay attention to all incoming information, it does a good job of filtering out that which is not important. The brain filters out about 98% of all incoming information. The good news is that the brain helps us to survive by effectively ruling out that which is not important. If we were to remember every experience that we have, we would all be anxious and fearful: We would not, for example, want to go outside because we would remember every near miss with a wasp, every bad experience with the weather. The brain does a great job of filtering out what we do not need to remember and, in so doing, keeps us from becoming phobic.

The bad news is that when our students do not perceive the information to be important, they may toss it out from the beginning.

GETTING THE BRAIN'S ATTENTION

We do not want to keep the brain's attention indefinitely, because we know that real learning comes in those times when students practice learning, process the information, and make it their own. According to Jensen (1997), requiring the brain's attention for long periods of time, as we do in the classroom, is not brain friendly. We know that our brains do not do well in situations where we must listen for long periods of time. All of us who have been in long meetings know that our attention fades in and out throughout the lecture. The same is true of our students. In my book *Ten Best Teaching Practices* (Tileston, 2000), I recommend using the students' age as a guide to how many minutes they will pay attention. If the students are twelve years old, do not talk more than twelve minutes at a time. For adults, twenty minutes seems to be the magic number.

In Chapter 2, we discussed the processes going on within the self-system of Mr. Trevino's students' brains as he stands to begin the class. In this chapter, we will discuss getting students' attention and helping them to use their innate drive to learn.

Most information (about 98%) comes to the learner through the senses. Once the brain perceives this incoming information, there is only a matter of seconds (perhaps as few as 15 seconds) in which the brain decides whether to pay attention or discard the information. Figure 3.1 is a simple visual model of how the information comes into the brain for processing.

The self-system, as the beginning point for learning, plays an important role as information is coming into the brain. The self-system decides whether to pay attention to the information being provided through the senses and to move it along to the cognitive system.

Figure 3.1   Incoming Information

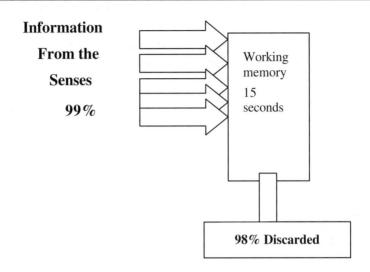

In Chapter 2, three important aspects of the self-system were introduced: interest, efficacy, and emotional response. In order to identify how to bring motivation into the classroom, it is important to look at each of these in terms of what happens as the brain makes decisions about the learning.

How Do We Satisfy the Self-System's Need for Positive Emotion?

Emotion is the strongest force for embedding information into the brain's long-term memory; it has the power to shut down our thinking or to strengthen an experience so that we remember it for life. We add emotion to the learning through sound (try adding music to lessons), celebrations of the learning, visuals, simulations, and real-world applications. My brother, who majored in pharmacy and works for a major drug company, told me recently that everything he ever needed to know to be successful he learned in second grade. His second-grade teacher, Mrs. Eggars, understood how to use emotion in the classroom brilliantly. He told me that when all of the other second-grade classes were studying a country, such as Italy, that they brought in some of the food of that country one day, showed some of the costumes another day, and so forth. Not so in his classroom; his classroom *was* Italy. It looked like, smelled like, tasted like, and sounded like Italy. Mrs. Eggars even introduced them to Italian opera. According to Jensen (1997),

> When the learner's emotions are engaged, the brain codes the content by triggering the release of chemicals that single out and mark the experience as important and meaningful. Emotions activate many areas in the body and the brain, including the prefrontal cortices, amygdala, hippocampus and often the stomach.

Brain researcher Robert Cloninger (in Jensen, 1997) says that to get the brain's attention we must tap into three neural systems. First, we must stimulate the quest for novelty, which comes from the cerebral cortex; second, we must trigger the hunt for pleasure, which comes from the midbrain; and third, we must activate the desire to avoid harm, which comes from the lower brain. Jensen (1997) says, "This analysis provides a perfect summary of our daily lives—try new things, seek pleasure and avoid getting hurt. We can use these rules of the brain to get student's attention when appropriate."

How Do We Use
Novelty to Get the Brain's Attention?

Novelty is used effectively with all of us daily. For example, imagine we are watching the news waiting for the weather to come on so that we can plan a trip. Just before the weather forecast airs, the weather reporter comes on to say, "Big changes coming in the weather this weekend, stay tuned for details." Then the commercial comes on. We don't dare change the channel for fear that we will miss the big changes that we definitely need to know about. The weather reporter has our attention. He has used emotional states tied closely to novelty—suspense and curiosity. Some other emotional states that help to get our student's attention include the following:

- Anticipation

- Hope

- Fun

- Acceptance

- Surprise

- Self-confidence

- Intrigue

- Importance

WHAT IS THE ROLE OF SELF-ATTRIBUTES?

Self-attributes include such things as one's beliefs about personal physical appearance, intellectual ability, athletic ability, and social ability. The combination of these beliefs constitutes one's overall self-concept. The phrase *locus of control* refers to the extent to which a person believes he or she has control over a situation (internal control) as opposed to the control of other people or forces outside of themselves (external control). Students who come to us from poverty often believe that they have no control over their lives or their circumstances. When students have lived with this idea over time, they often have low self-esteem and may have developed a feeling of helplessness. Payne (2001) says that in generational poverty, "Destiny and fate are the major tenets of the belief system. Choice is seldom considered."

Caine and Caine (1997) and McCune, Stephens, and Lowe (1999) say that students usually attribute their success or failure to one or more of the following: ability ("I'm just not smart"), effort ("I tried really hard"), task difficulty ("That test was too hard"), or luck ("I guessed right"). Many students have the overriding belief that what happens in life is just fate: They have no control.

McCune et al. (1999) add, "Researchers believe that students will be more likely to engage in learning activities when they attribute success or failure to things they can control, like their own effort or lack of it, rather than to forces over which they have little or no control, such as their ability, luck or outside forces." Teachers should help students, especially at-risk learners, to link their successes to something they did to contribute to the success. When teachers do this, the students develop self-efficacy and the confidence that they have the power within themselves to be successful.

What Is the Role of the Self and Others?

One area of the self-system involves the student's perception of the nature of formal and informal groups and their relationship to other individuals. We all want to belong somewhere. What we believe our status to be in those groups—whether at home, with peers, or within a certain club or organization—determines our sense of acceptance. Learned helplessness is a condition that over time affects motivation. It is based on an experience or experiences in which the student felt he or she had no control. Students who come from poverty or abuse have a tendency to believe they have no control.

Learned helplessness can be overcome by building into our lessons opportunities for success and by teaching students basic emotional intelligence strategies, such as goal setting. Try doing a class survey to find out what kinds of things your students like and what piques their interest. Build lessons and projects around student interests and provide explicit feedback often. What causes students to feed machines with quarters even when they are not very skillful at the activity— instant gratification and constant feedback?

WHAT IS THE ROLE OF THE STUDENT'S PERCEPTION OF THE NATURE OF THE WORLD?

Another area of the self-system deals with the individual's perception of the nature of the world, both in physical and sociological terms, including beliefs about why specific events occur. "These [perceptions] will include [the student's] beliefs about physical, emotional, sociological and supernatural forces, and how [these forces] came to affect specific situations and events" (Marzano, 1998). Do students believe in a hostile or friendly world? Stress causes the brain to trigger a reaction of defensiveness or a sense of helplessness. Jensen (1997) says that it is not stress that is bad, but rather uncontrollable stress: "Under such conditions, the brain may go into a 'survivalize' mode in which it becomes less capable of planning, pattern-detection, judgment skills, receiving information, creativity, classifying data, problem-solving and other higher-order skills."

Threats

We all experience fear or threat from time to time. Most researchers divide threats into various types based on their source. Here are some of the types of threats that our students face.

Threat of Bodily Harm—from classmates, from school personnel, even from family members. While the teacher cannot control all of the threats to students, the teacher who cruises the room, who talks to students, and who constantly provides feedback to students is more likely to identify and stop threats in his own classroom.

Threats Based on What We Do or Do Not Know About Learning. Students can feel threatened when their ideas are attacked, they receive derogative comments, they are given little or no fee back, or they are not provided with enough direction to complete a task. In order for students to be successful, they need specific directions, adequate opportunities to practice learning, and specific feedback for improvement. They also need to know before tackling an assignment what the expectations of the teacher are. No assignment should be given to students without a rubric or matrix telling them exactly what is expected. For young children, without reading skills, the directions should be simple and specific and should include teacher modeling.

In our restructured school, one of the first things that we did to change the climate within the school was to give students a matrix every time that we assigned a task for which we would take a grade. There was a time when I would say to my students, "I want you to do this at a quality level." What I soon found was that what I consider to be a quality level and what they consider to be a quality level were very different. By giving them a matrix that showed specifically what I wanted, I was able to raise the quality level of their work considerably. I believe that students would do work at a quality level more often if they knew what we meant by that phrase. Table 3.1 is a simple model that could be used for any project. On the left side, list the components of the task. On the right side, list the attributes that make the parts quality. In the center, list the point value of each of the components of the task.

Emotional Threats. Students fear being made to look foolish in front of their peers. Anything that causes them to feel inadequate, silly, stupid, hurt, or embarrassed will be an emotional threat. One of my college students told me a horrific story about an incident that took place in her school. An elementary teacher wanted to "motivate" her students to read more books so she set up a system of rewards for the number of books read. When students had read a given number of books, they were eligible to participate in a party to which parents were invited. On the appointed day of the party, only one student had not reached her quota of books and was not allowed to participate in the party. (The child was in attendance at the party, however, because it took place during school time.)

Table 3.1   Matrix for a Short Story

Components	Point Value	Attributes
Title		❏ Relates to the theme ❏ Grabs the attention
Theme		❏ Developed through patterns ❏ Developed through symbols ❏ Use of allusions ❏ Related to plot
Setting		❏ Adds value to the plot, characters, or theme
Characters		❏ Includes physical traits ❏ Dialogue use ❏ Actions ❏ Opinions ❏ Point of view ❏ Adequately developed
Point of view		❏ Appropriate to the story
Plot		❏ Well developed ❏ Complexity ❏ Climax ❏ Resolution

Parents were there, and everyone except this one child took part in the party. This teacher believed that by using a system of rewards and punishments she could coerce students into reading. What do you think the child who was left out of the party thinks of reading and of the classroom?

Threats Based on Bias. When students' names are made fun of or deliberately mispronounced, when students are isolated in hallways or in corners of the room, or when they are taught in only one modality, students feel threatened in the classroom. English language learners often become shy in classes, where they are afraid to speak up because of their poor English skills. These students also may feel threatened by unrealistic deadlines or lack of adequate resources to complete the task. Jensen (1997) says,

> Most so-called "at-risk" learners are in a constant state of stress or threat. As a result they constantly make choices that are biologically driven; that work for the short-term and are survival-oriented. They are not unmotivated or shortsighted. But the part of the brain that needs to be engaged for long-term planning (the parietal and frontal lobes of the cortex) are likely to have less blood flow and be less efficient. Educators that deal with these issues with awareness will find more long-term success than those who respond with a knee-jerk reaction that demands more discipline and higher standards.

How Does Climate Affect Motivation?

Climate refers to both the physical and emotional aspects of a classroom. Students need to feel comfortable in the classroom—both physically and emotionally.

Physical Climate

Stand at the door of your classroom. What do you see? Hear? Smell? What about your room appeals to students as they enter? How have you used such emotions as curiosity, acceptance, anticipation, security, and a sense of fun to make the room a pleasant place in which to be? To create an appealing atmosphere, try using music in your classroom when appropriate. Music has a tremendous impact on our emotions and it helps us remember. If you are teaching history or languages, bring in music from the time period or the place you are studying. Bring in room fresheners or gel candles (that do not have to be lit) to give the room a clean, fresh smell. If you are allowed, change the color of the room, change the lighting so that it is more natural, and change the room arrangement for the activities that you will be using. For example, for discussion, put the desks in a circle or horseshoe; for small group discussions, use small circles; and for debates, place the desks facing each other.

Emotional Climate

A positive emotional climate includes the following aspects.

Acceptance by the Teacher. Students need to believe that what they have done in the past does not matter: that they have a chance to be successful. Hope is what motivates us to continue a project, our work, a relationship. Students need to have the hope that they can be successful in the eyes of the teacher. One of the ways that a teacher helps students to feel accepted is to give them frequent and specific feedback on their work—not the general "nice job," but *specific* feedback. Another way that the teacher shows acceptance is by treating students with respect and with consistency.

Acceptance by Peers. Students need to feel safe in the classroom, and they need to believe that they will not be harmed, either physically or emotionally. Teachers create that sense of safety by setting class norms that include a "no put-downs" policy and by calling everyone by their first name or "name of choice." At the beginning of each semester in my classroom, I conduct some activities specifically designed to help my students know one another. I might have them interview a partner and introduce that partner to the rest of the group. I might have them work in groups of three to find things that they have in common, such as favorite sports, favorite dessert, or kinds of pets at home (I give them a list of topics to get them started).

A Sense of Order. The brain likes novelty, but it also likes order. Novelty without order is chaos. Students want to know that the way you grade their papers today is the same way that you will grade them tomorrow. They expect discipline problems to be taken care of immediately and with as little disruption as possible. Never ignore poor behavior; to do so is to send a signal to your students that order and discipline is not important. Create routines in your classroom and then add novelty to the lessons for flavor.

Clarity of Tasks. Students need to understand the directions they are given and need adequate time and rehearsal before performing tasks or before providing information for assessment. Temporary confusion helps us to learn when it is followed with opportunities to find the answers. However, confusion, over time, is frustrating and leads to demotivation. Caine and Caine (1997) suggest teachers create a classroom where there is a relaxed awareness, where there is low to moderate stress and high challenge. To accomplish that, we must create classrooms in which students feel comfortable about the learning and where they know it is all right if they do not know all the answers. In such a classroom, all are learners together, including the teacher.

Resources for Success. Students need to believe that they have the physical and mental resources necessary to be successful. Such resources include not only books, computers, and materials, but also time and adequate opportunities to practice the learning.

Emotional Intelligence. We can directly teach skills to our students that will build their emotional intelligence. This is a great starting place for training our students to use the self-system of the brain to help them begin and finish tasks.

In *Emotional Intelligence* (1995), author Daniel Goleman describes the profound and diverse impact that emotions have on our lifestyle. Goleman describes five main domains of emotional intelligence:

1. Knowing One's Emotions: This involves self-awareness so that one knows and recognizes an emotion as it happens. As Goleman says, "An inability to notice our true feelings leaves us at their mercy."

2. Managing Emotions: Students need to learn to handle emotions so that they are appropriate in terms of intensity and type. If you teach inner-city students whose lives on the street are surrounded by emotions—many of them negative—you will want to teach them some self-management skills. As Goleman says, "People who are poor in this ability are constantly battling feelings of distress, while those who excel in it can bounce back far more quickly from life's setbacks and upsets."

3. Motivating Oneself: Being able to focus emotions on a worthwhile goal is important in self-motivation, in paying attention, for mastery, and for creativity. Emotional self-control means that we can delay gratification and stifle impulsiveness in order to accomplish goals. Impulsiveness is what keeps our students from finishing tasks. Control of impulsiveness is valued by our society and is often the way in which intelligence is measured. When we constantly provide outside rewards for learning and behavior, we prevent students from developing this sense of self-motivation.

4. Recognizing Emotions in Others: Empathy is an important social skill that helps the learner to be more attuned to the needs and actions of others.

5. Handling Relationships: Being able to manage the emotions in others is an important skill. The ability to handle relationships is the underpinning of leadership, interpersonal effectiveness, and popularity.

As Goleman writes,

Until we acknowledge that we are, in fact, emotional beings and learn to deal constructively with that reality, we'll continue to have more problems. Our emotional illiteracy is related to discipline problems, dropout rates, low self-esteem and dozens of other learning and life skill problems. In order to progress, our culture has to take emotions out of the closet of the 'mysterious' and put them onto the table for discussion. Once people feel safe enough to talk about emotions, it will be easier to work with them. While emotional illiteracy can ruin families, finances and health, emotional literacy can lead to a rich, happy and satisfying life.

HOW IS IMPORTANCE RELATED TO MOTIVATION?

Most of us are on overload these days, so it stands to reason that if we cannot see the importance in something—and not just the importance, but also the *personal* importance—we are less likely to pay attention. I might believe that it is important for my best friend to learn physics because he is a scientist who uses a variety of science skills in his daily work. I believe physics is important, but that does not mean that I will accompany my friend to his advanced physics class. It is not important to me personally at this point. So, we must help our students to see the importance of the work and the relevance to them personally.

Jensen (1998) says, "In order for learning to be considered relevant, it must relate to something the learner already knows. It must activate a learner's existing neural networks. The more relevance, the greater the meaning." For example, a teacher introducing the book *Snowed in at Pokeweed Public School*, by Bianca, might begin by asking students what they would do if they had to spend the night at school. The teacher might give them some choices, such as playing games, singing, doing art activities, or crying for their parents. These are the same choices the students at Pokeweed face when they are snowed in overnight. By making the learning relevant to the students first, the teacher has opened the way for better understanding by the students. To begin a unit on estimation, a teacher might bring to class a jar of marbles, such as might be part of a contest to guess the number of marbles in the jar for a prize. Begin by asking the students for ideas about how to estimate the number in the jar. By doing this, the teacher has tapped into two very important emotions—curiosity, and fun.

WHY IS EFFICACY IMPORTANT TO MOTIVATION?

Part of the self-system concerns the extent to which a student believes that she or he has the resources or power to change a situation. A student can have a strong sense of efficacy in some situations and very little in others. A low sense of efficacy can result in learned helplessness.

Sprenger (2002) suggests some other tactics for helping students to feel in control of their learning. She suggests that teachers

- Provide opportunities for students to write their own ideas and feelings about the learning through journaling, learning logs, or discussions.
- Provide an agenda for the day or class so that students know what to expect and have predictability.

What Can You Do?

The questions below are meant to guide you in identifying areas of weakness in your classroom or school.

What are some things that you can do to assure that your students . . .

- Feel accepted by the teacher and their peers?
- Perceive the classroom as a comfortable and orderly place?
- Experience the learning through the senses?
- Perceive that this is their classroom and that they are part of the learning?
- Believe that they have some control over their learning?

4

How Do We Encourage Students to Finish the Task?

So many times as teachers, we believe we have finally made progress when we get reluctant students to begin a task only to be disappointed when they throw up their hands and quit at the first sign of problems. While the self-system helps students to pay attention to the learning and the task at hand, it is the metacognitive system that is paramount in leading students to complete procedural tasks.

ACTIVATING THE METACOGNITIVE SYSTEM

The metacognitive system comes into play once students have decided to become involved in learning. Important aspects of this system include setting personal goals for learning and a process for achieving the learning goals. The metacognitive system also monitors and adjusts as the learning takes place. Effectively enabling this system provides a greater surety that students will complete the tasks, even when they become difficult. The components of the metacognitive system are organized into four categories: (1) goal specification, (2) process specification, (3) process monitoring, and (4) disposition monitoring.

Goal Specification

The goal specification portion of the metacognitive system will take the goal passed down from the self-system and determine the approach or plan necessary to carry out that goal. For example, Mr. Trevino is discussing parts of speech in his language arts class. A student who has decided within the self-system that this is important for him to know and understand this subject has passed this goal to the metacognitive system. He decides that he will take notes now and then use those notes later in completing the tasks Mr. Trevino has assigned. Similarly, an elementary student may decide to make a chart of the multiplication facts to help her remember that information. In the meta-analysis studies by the Mid-continent Regional Educational Laboratory (McREL), Marzano (1998) says that the learning goals must be very specific and that when a teacher allows students to have some control over their own learning goals, a student at the 50th percentile can be moved to the 84th percentile. That is powerful.

When working with students from poverty, remember that characteristics often associated with the poor and urban poor include the inability to "focus attention and see objects in detail" (Payne, 2001). They are more likely to see the "big picture" rather than specifics. As a teacher, you may want to help your students to see the specific details of the task at hand. In Chapter 3, you were given a matrix for writing a short story. This is the kind of detail that needs to be taught to students if they are going to be able to adequately plan for completion of a project.

A teacher can specifically teach this aspect of motivation by first setting his or her own goals. Before beginning a unit of study, determine which state or national standard or standards you will be teaching. For example, for a unit on vocabulary, Mr. Trevino used these state goals:

Language Arts Standard 1: Demonstrates competence in the general skills and strategies of the writing process.

Language Arts Standard 2: Uses grammatical and mechanical conventions in written compositions.

Next, Mr. Trevino sets benchmarks or activities that he would use to measure his student's progress. For example,

Standard Two: Uses grammatical and mechanical conventions in written compositions.

Benchmark: Uses adjectives in written compositions (e.g., indefinite, numerical, predicate adjectives).

From the standards and the benchmarks, Mr. Trevino sets declarative objectives (what students will know) and procedural objectives (what students will be able to do) for the learning. Those objectives might look something like this:

Declarative Objectives: Students will know (1) the definitions of terms *adjective, indefinite adjective, numerical adjective,* and *predicate adjective*; (2) the appropriate use of each of the each type of adjective; and (3) how adjectives add value to writing

Procedural Objectives: Students will be able to (1) demonstrate appropriate use of each type of adjective by using them in written and verbal exercises; (2) use adjectives appropriately in their writing; and (3) use adjectives to add value to their writing.

Mr. Trevino displayed the standards, benchmarks, and objectives in the classroom and discussed them with the students prior to the learning. Then, Mr. Trevino asked the students to set personal goals for the learning. During the unit, Mr. Trevino frequently referred to the objectives he and the students had written to help students identify their own progress.

For young students who do not read yet, send the standards and benchmarks home to parents in a parent letter. Ask students to draw or tell something they want to learn.

For goal specification when learning a single set of facts or for carrying out a single task, the student might visualize the finished work to help him or her strategize how to carry out the task. A basketball player who has never visualized himself shooting a basket will probably have difficulty completing that task.

Process Specification

Process specification is assigned the function of identifying or activating the specific skills, tactics, and processes that will be used in accomplishing the goal passed on by the self-system. If a student has practiced the specified learning goal previously, process specification may come easily. However, if the goal passed on by the self-system is a new learning task, the student will need consciously to work out a strategy for success.

For example, assume an individual has determined that she will engage in the task of doing her math homework: She might set a strategy of working the problems that she knows how to do first, then taking on the more challenging problems later. Assuming that the individual knows how to work the math problems, the process specification simply retrieves from memory the steps and general rules that apply to multiplication. However, if she has never worked these types of problems before, the process specification function must determine not only which algorithms, tactics, and processes to use, but in what order they will be executed. This type of routine requires more conscious thought than those routines that are familiar and are therefore done by "automatic thought" processes. Students must be taught how to identify the steps necessary to accomplish a given task. Provide a variety of problem-solving techniques to your students so that they can make good choices about how to complete a task.

Process Monitoring

Process monitoring, as the name suggests, monitors the processes being used in the task. This function makes decisions about the rules and timing of the task. If the plan generated under goal specification breaks down, process monitoring asks for a new or revised plan. In the example of the math problems discussed above, this might involve asking for help or getting more information. Feedback, both positive and negative, is information given to students in regard to their work or behavior. The feedback might be verbal or written, and it might be in any of the following formats:

1. Notes taken by the teacher during observations (sometimes called *anecdotal records*).

2. General verbal or written statements given to the whole group in reference to an activity. For example, after students have worked in groups of three, the teacher might debrief the group on how well they worked together.

3. Comments or grades given by the teacher on work turned in.

4. Reflection activities in which students evaluate their own work.

5. Comments or written evaluations completed by group members after a group activity.

6. Activities, such as projects, in which there are several steps.

Students may self-evaluate and/or the teacher may evaluate the work by providing explicit feedback. It is important to note here that general feedback, such as "good job" or "nice writing," has very little positive impact on learning. It is explicit feedback that makes a difference, according to meta-analysis data. An example of explicit feedback might be, "The format you chose for your writing meets all of the criteria for persuasive writing" or "You left out Step Two in your calculations, and that is why you were not able to get the correct answer."

The teacher should directly teach another type of feedback called *self-talk*, because it is a powerful tool for all students and in particular students from poverty. Self-talk is the way in which we encourage or discourage ourselves verbally, and it is tied to self-concept. Students who have grown up in poverty usually have engaged in a great deal of negative self-talk, but often do not know how to use positive self-talk to help them finish a task. We help build resiliency in our students by teaching them to self-talk in a positive way when working through problems or learning that is difficult. Help move students away from such defeatist statements as "I'm stupid" or "I can't do this."

Demonstrate to students how you use self-talk as you work through a problem. What do you do when you come up against a brick wall? How do you talk yourself through day-to-day problems? Teach students to reflect on what they did right, what they did that worked, what didn't work, how could they have done something differently, how they could have made something neater or easier to understand. Students need to know that we all use self-talk to get ourselves through problems and daily activities. *Explicitly* teach them how to do this.

Disposition Monitoring

Disposition monitoring has to do with students' ability to monitor their own work and make changes or ask for help when needed. Marzano (2001) provides an example of disposition monitoring that he calls "clarity": Does the student know when the directions were not clear to him or his understanding was not accurate? Approaching a problem from the standpoint of clarity and accuracy is a conscious act, and students need to be taught to do this. Costa (1991) says that this part of the learning process is associated with "intelligent behavior."

For teachers, disposition monitoring involves providing students with wait time and with the necessary resources to carry out a procedural task. Using appropriate and adequate wait time can move a student from the 50th percentile in terms of understanding to the 70th percentile (Marzano, 1998).

The following dispositions might be included in this monitoring.

Accuracy. How well did the student do in terms of the assignment directions? In Chapter 3, we discussed why it is important to give students a model so that they can define quality. A matrix or rubric helps students to identify the accuracy with which they are completing the assignment.

Energy Given to the Task. Students need to identify whether they gave the task their best effort or merely walked through the steps. Students often begin a task with enthusiasm but become tired or uninterested as the task becomes more difficult. Frequently, students will turn in a product that is below expectations or one that is only half finished. Sloppy work or inattention to detail are also indicators that students are not putting forth their best efforts. In order to encourage students to finish their work at a quality level, we can offer specific feedback as they work. The feedback must be specific, diagnostic as well as prescriptive, and given often. Telling students that they did a great job when, in fact, they did not do their best can actually lower their learning abilities. In the studies identified by Marzano at McREL (1998), constructive feedback had one of the highest effects on student learning.

Restraint of Impulsivity. Students who do not finish tasks or who finish with minimum effort need direct instruction on controlling impulsivity. Impulsivity is one of the reasons students from poverty and inner-city poverty may not finish tasks. Their world outside of school often revolves around instant gratification and acting before thinking. Feedback is necessary for these students to help them control impulsivity. When they give up or act impulsively, ask them to write down what happened, what they did, and what they can do differently next time in order to be successful. The teacher must give them specific examples of other alternatives to acting on impulse, since these behaviors may not have been taught previously.

WHAT ABOUT MINOR OFF-TASK BEHAVIOR?

We all have experienced those times when we are bored, tired, or not being taught appropriately. For students, these feelings sometimes manifest themselves in off-task behavior, from tapping a pencil to talking to a neighbor. Jensen (1998) calls our actions and reactions to the learning *learning states*. Jensen (1997) identifies learning states in this way:

> A [learning] state is a distinct body-mind moment composed of a specific chemical balance in the body. The presence or absence of norepinephrine, vasopressin, ACTH, testosterone, serotonin, progesterone, dopamine and dozens of other chemicals dramatically alter your frame of mind and body. Our states are affected by: (1) our thoughts—mental pictures, sounds and feelings; and (2) our physiology—posture, breathing, gestures, eye patterns, digestion, and temperature.

The best state for learning depends on the material and learning objectives; however, some desirable states for learning are

- *Curiosity*: Use lead-in questions or statements to make your students know more. "There is going to be a fight between two rival gangs tonight. Want to know who wins? Read pages 328–340 in *Romeo and Juliet* and be ready to rumble (discuss it) tomorrow."
- *Anticipation*: I love to end my classes by saying, "Oh, by the way, when you come back to class . . ." and then giving them a teaser about something that we are going

to do. I want students to come to my door at 8:00 in the morning to find out what we are going to do at 2:00 in the afternoon. For one thing, my students never know where their desks will be. I change the room based on what we are going to do. If we are debating, the desks will either be in rows facing one another or they will be in two circles—an inside circle and an outside circle. If we are discussing together, the desks or chairs will be in a horseshoe or circle.

- *Suspense*: Provide challenges to your students or ask "what if" to raise the suspense level about the learning.
- *Low to moderate anxiety* (never high): Challenging work that involves higher-level thought will provide some temporary anxiety while the student formulates a plan for carrying out the work. Teachers must explicitly teach students how to plan and how to choose tools for problem solving.
- *High challenge*: One of the major reasons that students tune out is because the work is boring and/or they do not see the relevance. One of my favorite math teachers has a sign in her room that says, "I will never teach you anything in this room that I cannot tell you how it is used in the real world." It is a promise she keeps, and students are allowed to challenge her on it.
- *Low to moderate stress*: Again, when we are challenged, there is some stress, but when we know that we have the ability and resources to do the work, the stress is low to moderate, never high.
- *Temporary confusion* (not knowing all the answers so that we have to search for information): We cannot possibly teach students everything that they will need to know in life; we must teach them the basics and give them the ability to find answers for themselves.

Behavior that is not appropriate to the assignment is considered to be off task. There is a tendency by teachers to treat all off-task behavior as a discipline problem, but most off-task behaviors are a result of the brain's learning state. Jensen (1997) says to change the state of the learner, and then deal with the behavior. By making the learning meaningful, interesting, and unique, we are better able to prevent off-task behavior.

Next time your students exhibit off-task behavior (which is not to be confused with demotivation), try one of the following responses:

■ *Change the activity*: Sometimes just changing from one activity to another or going from individual to group work will change the learning state of students. I use this often when doing all-day seminars. I watch the body language of the people I am training to know when to give breaks, when to change activities, and when to pick up the pace.

■ *Change the environment*: Changing the lighting, the temperature, or the seating arrangement can often make a big difference in student attention. Using aromas and music can also have a profound affect. Remember, 99% of what we learn comes to us through the senses.

■ *Change the way you are presenting the information*: If you have been doing most of the talking, have students talk or bring in PowerPoint slides, computers, or other media to break up the lesson.

■ *Change who is doing the teaching*: Let students take segments of the lesson or bring in a guest speaker. If neither of these options is possible, change your speaking tone or the tone of the lesson.

■ *Change the working environment*. Change the amount of time students have to complete the work, or change the rules, the goals, the resources, or the method of obtaining information.

5

A Model for Developing Motivation in the Classroom

I n the preceding chapters, we have examined many factors that affect motivation. Now, let's put the information from those chapters together in a classroom setting to determine how a teacher can motivate students to learn.

First, we have said that the attitude toward and perception of learning is critical to building intrinsic motivation. Students must feel that they are a part of the learning environment and that they have a strong internal locus of control over their learning. Teachers help students do this by providing information in a variety of ways so that it reaches all learners. For example, many inner-city poor learn through stories and dialogue, and English language learners need visual stimulus and teaching in context, because they do not have the language acquisition skills needed to process the vocabulary of the learning. When teachers teach to all learners this way, it is called *pluralism*, because the teacher is using a variety of methods (plural methods) to reach all learners.

Shanna Walker is a teacher in an urban middle school. Ms. Walker has several students in her classroom who day-dream or work on other class work while she is teaching. After examining the research on motivation, Ms. Walker has decided to walk through the processes that help to facilitate motivation in the classroom and to ask herself some questions about her own classroom. She begins with the attitudes and perceptions about the learning, because she knows that this must be attended to first before she can teach her students.

ATTITUDES TOWARD AND
PERCEPTIONS OF THE LEARNING

Ms. Walker will move through a series of questions as she works to improve the motivation within her classroom.

What Can I Do to Assure That Students Feel Accepted by the Teacher and Their Peers?

In my classroom, I will provide activities that help students to know one another, and I will set as a class rule that we must respect each other. How students work with each other will be a part of my students' daily grades. Students will be assigned to study groups for the six weeks, and I will chart their ability to work together. I will use Form 5.1 to monitor my student's ability to work with others, and I will provide feedback to my students about my observations.

From time to time, I will ask my students to self-evaluate how they believe they are progressing. Form 5.2 is one example of a tool I might use to help students self-evaluate.

When students work in groups, I will have the group evaluate their ability to work together using Form 5.3.

I will carefully construct questions so that they provide oppor-tunities for students to be successful, and I will provide wait time that is consistent from student to student.

I will respect my students' individual differences by bringing in a wide variety of materials that show different cultures, both males and females in meaningful occupations, and handicapped students (such as a student in a wheelchair) as important parts of society.

I will use a questionnaire such as the one provided in Form 5.4 to determine my students' interests and strengths, and will, to the extent possible, take into account my students' interests in planning lessons.

What Can I Do to Assure That Students Perceive the Classroom as a Comfortable and Orderly Place?

In my classroom, I will arrange my room according to the purpose of the lesson. For example, if we are discussing material, I will put the chairs in a horseshoe arrangement. If we are debating an issue, I will make rows facing each other. If my students are working in small groups of three, I will pull their desks together in a T shape.

Form 5.1   Student Behaviors

Student Name _____   Class Period _____

Point	M	T	W	Th	F
Week 1					
Week 2					
Week 3					
Week 4					
Week 5					
Week 6					

Legend: "+" indicates a positive behavior; "−" indicates a negative behavior

OT = on task

S = social skills (such as positive talk, working together, planning, etc.)

T = use of time and work turned in on time

Q = quality of the work

Form 5.2   Self-Evaluation

Answer the following questions about your work today:

1. Do you feel that you did your best work today?

2. If you had the time over again, what would you do differently?

3. Were you on task most (95%) of the time?

4. Did you have adequate directions to be successful?

5. Did you have the resources that you needed to be successful?

6. Did you encounter any problems?

7. What did you do to overcome the problems with the work?

8. Did you accomplish your personal goals for today?

My students will know, in advance, where homework goes when it is turned in, what the rules for restroom breaks or other needs are, and how to get my attention when there are questions or concerns.

I will provide class rules (made with my students' input) and directions for notebooks and such at the beginning of the semester or school year, and all rules will be posted in writing somewhere in the classroom. I will be consistent in maintaining those rules.

In addition, prior to a unit, I will give my students the objectives (which will be tied to state and local objectives) in writing, and I will put them up in the classroom so that throughout the unit my students can check their own progress in meeting the goals.

What Can I Do to Assure That Students Experience the Learning Through the Senses?

My room will be visually appealing with appropriate material on the walls, including examples of student work. The room will be clean and orderly.

Form 5.3   Collaborative Groups

Name of group:

Group members:

Six week period:

Skills for Daily Grade

Date	On Time	On Task	Quality	Social Skills

Form 5.4   Student Questionnaire

1. Do you like . . . [science, English, reading, etc.]?

2. What has been your experience with this subject before?

3. What was your favorite thing that you did in this subject in the past?

4. What would you like to learn in this class?

5. What kind of grade do you hope to receive in this class?

6. What can I do to help you to be successful?

7. If I promise to be the best teacher you have ever had, will you promise to be the best student in this subject that you have ever been before?

My room will smell clean and appealing. I will bring smells to the class that are appropriate to the lessons or that are generic, such as cinnamon or apples, by using unlit gel candles or sprays.

I will use music from time to time when it is appropriate to the learning, for celebrations, and sometimes for entering and leaving the classroom.

I will sometimes use taste when it is appropriate to the activity.

If it is okay with my supervisor or principal, I will allow my students to drink water in my classroom, since hydration is important to the brain. I will work within the politics of my school to assure that good nutrition is a part of the school breakfast and lunch program, and I will make my students aware of the impact of nutrition on the brain.

What Can I Do to Assure That Students Perceive That This Is Their Classroom and That They Are a Part of the Learning Process?

I will provide opportunities for students to give me feedback on the learning and on the general atmosphere in the classroom. I may use written or verbal feedback instruments. I will listen to my students openly and will make decisions after I have listened.

I will never give my students an assignment for which I am going to take a grade without first giving them a rubric or matrix that shows them my expectations. If the students meet the expectations, they get the grade. There are no "gotchas" in which students are graded on something for which they had no advance warning and they are not tested on anything that we have not studied. I will learn to use rubrics and will create rubrics for assignments. The following Websites may help me as I learn to use this powerful tool:

www.therubricator.com

www.inspiration.com

I will be fair and consistent in my treatment of my students and in my grading procedures.

LEARNING STATES AND DISCIPLINE PROBLEMS

After Ms. Walker was satisfied that the climate within her classroom was one that encouraged learning and intrinsic motivation, she looked at how she begins her lessons. Many of the discipline problems we encounter in the classroom are really learning-state problems and off-task behavior that can be changed by altering the learning state of the learners. Ms. Walker learned in her study on motivation that there are three ways that we get the brain's attention: (1) through patterns built on past learning or experiences, (2) through relevance, and (3) through emotion.

Usually Ms. Walker begins her lessons by calling for the class's attention, which also sometimes involves calling down students who are creating a disturbance. As Ms. Walker thought about her class, she thought about how her students enter the room from the hallway. Some of them were loud when entering, calling to each other; some of her students were not in their seats when the tardy bell rang, and some had their heads on their desks.

Ms. Walker decided to change the learning state the students have as they enter the room. She started to do so by placing her students into study groups of four, based, in part, on their personalities and their learning modalities. Within each group of four she attempted to place someone who was a leader, someone who was highly organized, someone who was a good communicator and someone who was creative. She also made sure that there was a mix of male and female students and of different ethnicities. Ms. Walker provided some activities to help the students get to know each other. She had several books that provide ideas for these activities, such as *Tribes, Joining Together,* and *Strategies for Teaching Differently.* One of the activities that she used is shown in Form 5.5. In this activity, students write down information about the other members of the group. This activity is a great way to show students ways they are alike and different.

Form 5.5   Team Building Activity: How Are We Alike?

TEAM

Members	Favorite Sport	Favorite Food	Favorite Class

How are you alike?

How are you different?

Ms. Walker explained that every time the students come to class they were to get into their study groups (unless a different direction was on the board) and were to discuss or work on the assignment that would be on the board. She told them that class begins when they walk into the room, not when the bell rings.

Ms. Walker also decided to begin each unit of study by creating a connection to what students already know. By doing this, she is providing personal relevance for her students. Sometimes, that would simply be discussing what they did the last time that class met or, for a new unit, that might mean providing activities that help students to see the real-world application of what they are doing. Furthermore, Ms. Walker made sure that students knew the relevance of the work. When appropriate, she added emotion to the lesson through music, costumes, laughter, and discussion.

Ms. Walker knew that once she had the students' attention, the neural systems would take over and the brain would decide whether to pay attention or not. She knew that she only had a matter of seconds to bring her students into the learning and to motivate the self-system to pay attention (see Figure 5.1).

The Self-System and the Metacognitive System

The self-system controls the metacognitive system. The self-system decides whether to pay attention to the information being provided through the senses; it also decides how much energy will be brought to the learning process. Some of the issues involved in the self-system, to which Ms. Walker must attend, include the following.

Examining the Importance of the Task. Ms. Walker knows that students must perceive that the task has meaning to them personally. Ms. Walker begins the unit by providing students with the objectives of the lesson and what they will learn. This information is posted in the room so that Ms. Walker can refer

Figure 5.1   Using the Neural Systems to Enhance Motivation

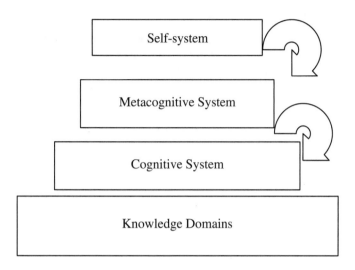

to it as the students work through the unit. For each new unit of study, Ms. Walker asks her students to write personal goals. Sometimes she does this by using a tool such as a KWLH (Know, Want to know, Learned, How I learned) form, like the one in Form 5.6. Using this tool, students write what they already know about the subject under the K. Then, under the W, they write personal goals for the learning. (Some teachers use N for *need to know* instead of the W.) At the end of the learning, students look back at what they wrote under the K and W, and write what they have learned under the L. Finally, under H, they write about how they learned what they listed under L. It is important for students not only to know *what* they know but also *how* they learned it. All of this helps to build positive self-efficacy.

Sometimes, Ms. Walker asks questions that students answer in their learning logs, and other times she may have students write goals based on a given format. She tells students that she will be reading and going over their personal goals and that the goals will be a part of the rubric

Form 5.6   KWLH

Know	Want to Know	Learned	How I Learned

for success on the unit. Ms. Walker provides a rubric for her students so that they know up front what is expected of them and what they will be doing.

Examining Efficacy. Ms. Walker knows that students need to believe that they have the resources, ability, or power to be successful on the given knowledge component. For that reason, Ms. Walker takes time to go over the learning matrix and to give thoughtful answers to students' questions. She watches body language and listens to questions and concerns to be sure that everyone understands the expectations. Ms. Walker encourages her students and makes them aware that she believes in them and that they can do work at a quality level.

Examining Emotions. Ms. Walker is aware that emotion is the strongest force in the brain and that positive emotion about a task can make all of the difference in the amount of effort put into completing that task. To introduce a new unit on fractions, Ms. Walker brings pizza dough to class and discusses how fractions are used in pizza. She also tells her students that since pizza is cut into fractional parts and sold that way, it is important for them to know the fractions in order to get the most for their money. (You can view a lesson like this in the PBS video series *Good Morning Ms. Toliver.* Check with your school librarian to see if your school has this wonderful series on math.)

The Metacognitive System and the Cognitive System

The metacognitive system can control any and all aspects of the knowledge domains and the cognitive system. The components of the metacognitive system are organized into four categories: (1) goal specification, (2) process specification, (3) process monitoring, and (4) disposition monitoring (discussed in more depth in Chapter 4).

Goal Specification. The goal specification portion of the metacognitive system will take the goal passed down from the self-system and determine its specifics. Ms. Walker set the stage for this process when she had students write personal goals for the lesson. She also will trigger goal specification by giving each student a piece of cardboard shaped like a pizza and another piece of cardboard to cut into fractional parts. The students will decorate their pizzas with toppings using crayons and colored paper, and then they will cut it according to the fraction assigned to their study group (e.g., $\frac{1}{4}$, $\frac{1}{8}$, $\frac{1}{16}$).

Process Specification. Process specification is assigned the function of identifying or activating the specific skills, tactics, and processes that will be used in accomplishing the goal. Students know what pizza looks like and they know the toppings that they prefer. If the students do not know fractional parts, Ms. Walker will need to provide that information prior to this activity; however, Ms. Walker's students have been studying fractional parts for some time and so know the basic fractions.

Process Monitoring. Process monitoring supervises the processes being used in the task. This function makes decisions about the heuristics, algorithms, and timing of the task. If the plan that was generated under goal specification breaks down, process monitoring asks for a new or revised plan.

Deposition Monitoring. Deposition monitoring addresses the extent to which the task is carried out in ways that optimize the effectiveness of the algorithms, tactics, and processes being used. This function monitors how one approaches the task that has been selected. Aspects of disposition that it supervises include

- Accuracy and precision of the task at hand ("How well am I doing?")
- Clarity of task and purpose ("I understand the task, can formulate plans for completing the task, and can make adjustments as needed")
- Restraint of impulsivity (so that the task is done according to plan and so that the student does not give up when a problem is encountered in the process)
- Intensity of the task engagement (so that the task is completed with high energy and enthusiasm)
- Task focus (staying on task throughout the process)

Ms. Walker walks about the room as students work in their groups to make sure that they understand the fractional part that they have been assigned. Students are given feedback—from the teacher, their peers, and from themselves as they view their work—on how well they are doing. Ms. Walker knows that once a task is started, feedback is required for motivation to stay at a high level to completion of the task.

WHAT ARE SOME THINGS THAT
MS. WALKER DID TO REACH DIVERSE LEARNERS?

1. Ms. Walker taught fractions in context. Students love to eat and most students love pizza, so her context was the fractional parts that make up a pizza.

2. Ms. Walker had her students set personal goals. While this is important for all students, it is critical for diverse learners, because it makes the learning personal.

3. Rather than teach fractions by lecture or by reading the text, Ms. Walker helped her English language learners to a pathway that is more brain friendly for them than the semantic pathway, which is dependent on words. By providing movement and discussion, Ms. Walker appealed to the most comfortable type of learning environment for urban poor—kinesthetic.

4. Because it is so important to create a relationship and to create an environment that is threat-free for both poor and urban learners, Ms. Walker took care of the classroom environment first.

6

A Model for Facilitating Motivation

In Chapter 5, an example was provided for helping the classroom teacher understand motivation in students. This chapter provides a guide to help you as you work with your own students in facilitating motivation in your classroom. The following procedure can be used in any classroom to move students from a state of demotivation to one in which students are motivated to complete a task.

Choose a task that your students seem to have difficulty completing and walk through the questions below to help change your students from demotivated to motivated.

A MODEL FOR TURNING ON THE MOTIVATION WITHIN

Form 6.1 provides a model for changing demotivated students into motivated ones.

If demotivation is a major problem in your school, there are solutions—not quick fixes. Here are some questions

(text continues on page 64)

Form 6.1   Model for Changing Demotivation to Motivation

I. Attitudes and Perceptions About the Learning

Category	What Will You Do?
Ensure students feel accepted: • By the teacher • By peers in the room	
Ensure students perceive the classroom as comfortable and orderly	
Ensure students experience the learning through the senses	
Ensure students are a part of the learning process	
Ensure that my grading procedures are fair and consistent	

II. The Self-System

Category	What Will You Do?
Routines for beginning class	
Importance of the task	
Efficacy	
Positive Emotion	

(Continued)

Form 6.1 Continued

III. The Metacognitive System

Category	What Will You Do?
Goal specification	
Process specification	
Process monitoring	
Deposition monitoring	

IV. Changing Temporary Learning States

Learning-State Problem	What Will You Do?
The activity	
The environment	
Mode of presentation	
People	
Tone	

V. Working With Diverse Learners

Diverse Learners	What Will You Do?
Inner-city learners	
Students from generational poverty	
English language learners	

to ponder as you work through changing demotivation to motivation.

1. Have the teachers and administrators in your school been trained in the areas of cultural awareness, learning styles, and brain research?

2. Have the teachers and administrators in your school been trained to use resources (e.g., computers, peer helpers, various tools to teach to all student modalities) more effectively?

3. What has been done in your school to reduce language barriers?

4. Are students given choices?

5. What has been done to eliminate bias, sarcasm, and bullying?

6. Does your school emphasize proper nutrition and hydration?

7. Do you teach students emotional intelligence? Goal setting? Positive self-talk?

8. Do you provide feedback often and consistently?

Vocabulary
Summary

At-Risk Students

At-risk students are those who have one or more of the factors attributed to them that are usually connected with students who fail or who drop out of school. Broad categories usually include inner-city, low-income, and homeless children; those not fluent in English; and special-needs students with emotional or behavioral difficulties. Substance abuse, juvenile crime, unemployment, poverty, and lack of adult support are thought to increase a youth's risk factor.

Celebrations

Celebrations occur after the learning has taken place. Celebrations will either not have market value or not be expected. A pat on the back or a team cheer is a celebration. Celebrations are a form of extrinsic motivation.

To move students away from extrinsic rewards that are expected, use celebrations often in the classroom. Celebrate the learning with high fives, cheers, words of praise, and so forth.

Climate

Climate refers to both the physical and emotional effects of a classroom. Physical aspects of climate include such things as

- Room arrangement
- Appearance of the room
- Smell
- Temperature
- Lighting
- Time of day

Emotional aspects of climate include such things as

- Acceptance by the teacher
- Acceptance by peers
- The value the student places on the tasks
- The clarity of the tasks
- The resources available to be successful
- Self-esteem
- Locus of control
- A sense of order
- Lack of threat

Contextualization

Contextualization is a term that has emerged in the research on working with the urban poor and with certain ethnic groups. Within these frameworks, students learn through context better than they do by simply listening to a lecture or to general rules about how to do something. Most of what they have learned prior to coming to school has been in the context of experience, and thus they equate learning with the context of how or when it was learned.

Extrinsic Motivation

Extrinsic motivation is the desire to do something because of the promise or hope of a tangible result. Extrinsic motivation is a product of the behaviorist point of view that we can manipulate behavior by providing rewards and/or punishments. The father of this movement is generally thought to be Skinner, who conducted many experiments in which he provided rewards for desired behavior and punishments for undesired behavior (or the absence of desired behavior). Examples of common *extrinsic rewards* include

1. The promise of a candy if students will do their work, behave, listen, or do well on a test.

2. The offering of an eraser if a student will behave well in class.

3. The regular gift of a sticker to students who offer correct answers on a test.

Examples of *extrinsic incentives* that are not rewards (they have no material value) include

1. Free time for work well done.

2. Grades for quality work.

3. Pats on the back, thumbs up, and words of praise for good work or behavior.

Feedback

Feedback is the information, both positive and negative, given to a student in regard to their work or behavior. Research from Marzano (1998) shows that feedback that is consistent and specific has a strong effect on student success. Just saying "Good job" is not enough. Feedback must be diagnostic and prescriptive, deserved, and given often—some researchers say every thirty minutes.

Generational Poverty

Generational poverty refers to children who come from families that have lived in poverty over more than one generation. This is in contrast to *temporary poverty*, where the loss of a job or some disaster results in a temporary state of poverty.

Intrinsic Motivation

Intrinsic motivation is the desire to do something for the joy of doing it, learning it, or other intangible result.

Learned Helplessness

Learned helplessness is a condition that, over time, affects motivation. It is based on an experience or experiences in which the student felt he/she had no control. Students who come from poverty or abuse often have a tendency toward learned helplessness.

Learning State

A *learning state* is the mental and emotional state of the student in regard to learning. The best learning state is one in which the student is relaxed, has low to moderate stress, and is highly challenged.

Locus of Control

Locus of control refers to the extent to which a person believes he or she has control over a situation (*internal control*) as opposed to the control of other people or forces outside of themselves (*external control*). Students who come to us from poverty often believe that they have no control over their lives or their circumstances. When students believe this over time, they often have low self-esteem and may develop a feeling of helplessness.

Metacognitive System

The *metacognitive system* is the portion of the brain that seems to control all systems other than the self-system. It is this system that causes a student to follow through and to complete work with high motivation and energy.

Off-Task Behavior

Behavior that is not appropriate to the assignment is considered to be off-task.

Rewards

Rewards are a form of extrinsic motivation. In order to be classified as rewards, they will have two characteristics: They have *commercial value* and they *are expected.*

Self-Efficacy

The confidence a person has that he or she has the ability to be successful is called *self-efficacy.* The basic difference between self-efficacy and *self-esteem* is that, while both terms refer to the belief that one can be successful, self-efficacy is based on past experience.

Self-Esteem

Self-esteem is the value a person places on himself or herself. Sometimes this term is used interchangeably with *self-concept,* which is the way a person views himself or herself.

Self-System

The *self-system* of the brain is the gatekeeper to motivation. It is the self-system that first decides whether a student will pay attention and whether he or she will begin a task.

Self-Talk

Self-talk is the way in which we encourage or discourage ourselves verbally. Self-talk is tied to self-concept. We help build resiliency in our students by teaching them to self-talk when working through problems or learning that is difficult. Help move students away from defeatist statements such as, "I'm stupid" or "I can't do this."

Teacher Expectations

A teacher's perception of students' ability to be successful form the teacher's expectations. Early studies proved that students tend to do better or worse in school based on the teacher's expectations. Believing that all students can learn and truly setting your standards to that belief has a strong effect on student learning. Sometimes schools or individual classrooms will set a mastery standard at 75% or 85% based on what the staff expects students to be able to do on state and local exams. I have never set a mastery level of less than 100%. If I set a mastery level of 75% for my students, the question is, "Who are the students in that other 25%? Is it my child—or your child?" Casualties are light unless you are one of them. Don't give up on your students.

Threat

A *threat* is any stimulus that causes the brain to trigger a reaction of defensiveness or a sense of helplessness.

Wait Time

Wait time is the amount of time after a question is asked before the teacher moves to another student. Wait time should be three to five seconds, and it should be consistent.

Vocabulary Post-Test

At the beginning of this book, you were given a vocabulary list and a pre-test on that vocabulary. Below are the post-test and the answer key for the vocabulary assessment.

Vocabulary Post-Test

Instructions: Choose the one best answer for each of the questions provided.

1. Students who come to the classroom believing that nothing they do will be successful have most likely acquired . . .
   A. Locus of control
   B. Learned helplessness
   C. Meaning making
   D. Affective domain

2. Which of the following control initial motivation to listen to the teacher?
   A. Locus of control
   B. Metacognitive system
   C. Potential embarrassment
   D. Self-system

3. When a student perceives that he or she can be success-
ful based on past success, this is an example of . . .
   A. Extrinsic motivation
   B. Positive reinforcement
   C. Self-efficacy
   D. Meaning making

4. Which of the following learning states are *not* desirable?
   A. Suspense
   B. High anxiety
   C. High challenge
   D. Temporary confusion

5. Which of the choices below is an example of cultural/
social threat?
   A. Physical harm
   B. Potential embarrassment
   C. Disrespect
   D. Unreasonable deadlines

6. Which of the choices below is an example of intellec-
tual threat?
   A. Disrespect
   B. Unreasonable deadlines
   C. Incomplete directions given for a task
   D. Working by oneself

7. Self-efficacy is an important part of . . .
   A. Metacognition
   B. The self-system
   C. Physical needs
   D. Safety needs

8. Feedback . . .
   A. Should be positive only
   B. Should be constructive only
   C. Should be given in general terms such as "good
   job"
   D. Should be specific, positive, and constructive

9. Which of the following is not a condition for being at risk?
   A. Previous failure
   B. Low socioeconomic status
   C. Previous discipline problems
   D. Single parent home

10. Which of the following is not true of self-talk?
    A. It is usually done aloud.
    B. It can be negative.
    C. It can be positive.
    D. It is linked to student success.

11. Which of the following is an example of rewards?
    A. Students are told that they will be given stickers for good work.
    B. Students are provided with stickers after they do surprisingly well on a test.
    C. Students in groups give each other high-fives for completing their work.
    D. Students are praised by the teacher for their good behavior.

12. Most off-task behavior is the result of . . .
    A. Teacher behavior
    B. Difficult tasks
    C. A poor learning state
    D. The desire for attention

13. Which of the following is an example of a celebration?
    A. Students are praised by the teacher for their good behavior.
    B. Students are promised a pizza party for good behavior.
    C. Students are given the opportunity to win a bicycle for perfect attendance
    D. Students are promised and then given free time for good grades on the Friday test.

14. Which of the following is an example of resource restriction?
    A. An essay returned with derisive comments
    B. Isolation from peers during class
    C. An English language learner taught verbally
    D. A negative reward system

15. There are two categories of climate in the classroom: They are . . .
    A. Isolational and inclusive
    B. Emotional and physical
    C. Cultural and social
    D. Physical and mental

16. Which of the following is *not* an aspect of positive feedback?
    A. It is provided at least every 30 minutes.
    B. It is sincere.
    C. It is provided frequently.
    D. It is given whether earned or not.

17. Schools who use contextualization are . . .
    A. Usually working with special needs students.
    B. Teaching students from urban poverty.
    C. Teaching to the text.
    D. Teaching gifted students.

18. Which of the following statements is true of wait time?
    A. The amount of time varies with the learners.
    B. Clues should be given to help the learner remember.
    C. Brighter students should not be given as much time as slower students.
    D. Wait time should be the same for all learners.

19. *Locus of control* refers to . . .
    A. The extent that learners can control others.
    B. The extent that others can control the learner.
    C. How much control the learner perceives that he has.
    D. The teacher's ability to maintain order.

20. *Generational poverty* refers to . . .
    A. The loss of a job by the major breadwinner of the
       family.
    B. The loss of jobs by several generations of members
       of the family.
    C. An economic status caused by homelessness.
    D. An economic status over time.

VOCABULARY POST-TEST ANSWER KEY

1.	B	11.	A
2.	D	12.	C
3.	C	13.	A
4.	B	14.	C
5.	C	15.	B
6.	C	16.	D
7.	D	17.	B
8.	C	18.	D
9.	D	19.	C
10.	A	20.	D

References

Caine, R. N., & Caine, G. (1997). *Education on the edge of possibility.* Alexandria, VA: Association for Supervision and Curriculum Development.

Costa, A. L. (1991). Toward a model of human intellectual functioning. In A. L. Costa (Ed.), *Developing minds: A resource book for teaching thinking* (Rev. ed.). Alexandria VA: Association for Supervision and Curriculum Development.

Goleman, D. (1995). *Emotional intelligence: Why it can matter more than IQ.* New York: Bantam.

Jensen, E. (1997). *Completing the puzzle: The brain-compatible approach to learning* (2nd ed.). Del Mar, CA: Turning Point.

Jensen, E. (1998). *Introduction to brain-compatible learning.* Del Mar, CA: Turning Point.

Kohn, A. (1993). *Punished by rewards.* New York: Houghton Mifflin.

Marzano, R. J. (1992). *A different kind of classroom: Teaching with dimensions of learning.* Alexandria, VA: Association for Supervision and Curriculum Development.

Marzano, R. J. (1998). *A theory-based meta-analysis of research on instruction.* Aurora, CO: Mid-Continent Regional Educational Laboratory.

Marzano, R. J. (2001) *Designing a new taxonomy of educational objectives.* Thousand Oaks, CA: Corwin.

Maslow, A. H. (1968). *Toward a psychology of being.* New York: Van Nostrand Reinhold.

McCune, S. L., Stephens, D. E., & Lowe, M. E. (1999). *Barron's how to prepare for the ExCET* (2nd ed.). Hauppauge: NY: Barron's Educational Series.

Payne, R. K. (2001). *A framework for understanding poverty.* Highlands, TX: Aha! Process.

Sprenger, M. (2002) *Becoming a wiz at brain based teaching.* Thousand Oaks, CA: Corwin.

Sylwester, R. A. (1995). *Celebration of neurons: An educator's guide to the human brain*. Alexandria, VA: Association for Supervision and Curriculum Development.

Tileston, D. W. (2000). *Ten best teaching practices: How brain research, learning styles, and standards define teaching competencies*. Thousand Oaks, CA: Corwin.

Index

**CORWIN
PRESS**

The Corwin Press logo—a raven striding across an open book—represents the happy union of courage and learning. We are a professional-level publisher of books and journals for K-12 educators, and we are committed to creating and providing resources that embody these qualities. Corwin's motto is "Success for All Learners."